THE COLLEGE FOOTBALL CHAMPIONSHIP

The FIGHT for the TOP SPOT

Matt Doeden

M MILLBROOK PRESS · MINNEAPOLIS

Millbrook Press
A division of Lerner Publishing Group, Inc.
241 First Avenue North
Minneapolis, MN 55401 USA

For reading levels and more information, look up this title at www.lernerbooks.com.

Main body text set in Adobe Garamond Pro Regular 14/19
Typeface provided by Adobe Systems.

Library of Congress Cataloging-in-Publication Data

Doeden, Matt.
  The college football championship : the fight for the top spot / Matt Doeden.
      pages cm. — (Spectacular Sports)
    Audience: Age: 10–18.
    Audience: Grade: 7 to 12.
    ISBN 978-1-4677-1897-4 (lb : alk. paper) — ISBN 978-1-4677-8852-6 (eb pdf)
    1. Football—United States—History—Juvenile literature. 2. College sports—United States—History—Juvenile literature. I. Title.
  GV959.5.D64 2016
  796.332'63—dc23   2014041355

Manufactured in the United States of America
1 – VP – 7/15/15

CONTENTS

INTRODUCTION
CHAMPIONSHIP THRILLS

The crowd roars as the quarterback barks out his signals. He takes the snap. Shoulder pads crunch and helmets crash as the offensive and defensive lines clash. Camera flashes fill the stadium as the ball sails through the air and drops into the arms of a wide receiver racing down the sideline.

These are some of the sights and sounds of big-time college football. But this is no ordinary college football game. This is the national championship. Two teams. One trophy. Every down, every play, it's all on the line.

It's almost hard to believe that the national title game is relatively new in college football. For more than a century, the sport went on without such a spectacle. Championships were settled on paper rather than on grass and turf. But no longer. The College Football Playoff National Championship game answers a question that's as old as the sport: *Who's No. 1?*

Opposite page: The Ohio State Buckeyes celebrate their victory in the first College Football Playoff National Championship game in January 2015.

This drawing shows a rugby match between Yale and Columbia University.

1

WHO'S NO. 1?
A HISTORY OF COLLEGE FOOTBALL'S CHAMPIONSHIP

When a ragtag collection of rowdy athletes from Rutgers and Princeton met on the field for college football's first game in 1869, no one imagined the hugely popular tradition that the sport would become. In the early years, teams played without the expectation of a playoff or a title game to determine a champion. Yet fans must have asked the same question then that they ask today: Which team is the best in the land?

In 1869 the sport of college football was vastly different than it is in modern times. There were no scholarships, power conferences, or National Collegiate Athletic Association (NCAA) rules. It would be half a century before professional football leagues would offer college stars the chance of a career playing the sport. And even the game itself, designed as a cross between soccer and rugby, bore little resemblance to modern football. The game was played with a round ball and featured teams of 25 players on each side. The forward pass didn't exist, and the sport had few rules. Even so, fans and players had a blast at that first college football game. Rutgers beat Princeton in front of a small crowd, 6 – 4. A tradition was born.

THE EVOLVING GAME

Not until the early 1880s did college football begin to resemble the modern game. Former Yale player Walter Camp was dissatisfied with the disorganized nature of the sport. Camp set out to give structure to the game he loved. He introduced many of the rules that are still used. Camp's rules limited each team to 11 players on the field at a time. They established the practice of starting each play, or down, on a line of scrimmage that separated the offense from the defense. And the rules specified that teams would have a set number of downs to advance the football. Camp's original system allowed teams three downs to gain five yards, but it was later changed to the modern system of four downs to gain 10 yards.

The game thrived under the structure that Camp created. By 1900 football teams were sprouting up at universities all around the country. As the number of teams grew, so too did the rivalries that fans loved. The sport was on the rise, but early college football was a violent game played largely by brute force. Players were offered little protection by the rules or by the equipment. Injury and death were common. The 1905 season was a tipping point. With 18 confirmed deaths that season, even hard-core fans questioned the game. Columbia University—one of the first colleges to embrace football—banned the sport as too dangerous. Even President Teddy Roosevelt said that the sport was too brutal and urged change.

That December representatives from 62 schools met to talk about improving safety. Their goal was to preserve the excitement of the game while making it safer for players. The new rules they introduced—including the banning of the dangerous flying wedge play, in which masses of players charged headfirst into one another—accomplished just that. And for the first time, the rules allowed the forward pass, an innovation that would change the game forever.

Forward Thinking

When school representatives gathered in 1905 to revamp college football's rules, many media members, fans, and coaches focused on the plays that were banned to improve safety. But one rule change that initially received little attention would go on to completely change the game—the legalization of the forward pass.

At first, the rule change was barely noticeable during games. The forward pass was fraught with danger, and teams were rarely willing to attempt it. An incomplete pass resulted in a 15-yard penalty. And if a pass fell to the ground untouched, possession of the ball went to the other team! Few were willing to risk such dire consequences.

On September 5, 1906, Saint Louis University quarterback Bradbury Robinson chucked the first legal forward pass in organized football history, a 20-yard completion to Jack Schneider. Yet most coaches all but ignored the new type of play. Then, in 1907, Glenn "Pop" Warner of Pennsylvania's Carlisle Indian Industrial School built a playbook around the forward pass. Warner's offense also had a lot of trick plays, and the new playbook left opposing defenses confused and confounded. When Warner and his undersized Carlisle team defeated previously unbeaten powerhouse Pennsylvania, 26–6, other teams took notice. The forward pass was here to stay.

The 1906–1907 Saint Louis University football team.

CROWNING A CHAMPION

Modern-day statisticians have crowned college football champions going all the way back to 1869—titles that the NCAA formally recognizes. But in the early part of the 20th century, there was no official college football champion. Fans and reporters could argue over which team was the greatest. Various newspapers named national champions. Sometimes, schools simply declared themselves the champs. For decades, no official consensus acknowledged which team was the best in the land.

That changed in 1926, when University of Illinois economics professor Frank G. Dickinson devised a mathematical system to determine the nation's top college football team. The system considered factors such as a team's record and the quality of their opponents. After working through the season's numbers, Dickinson declared unbeaten Stanford to be the 1926 national champ. But there was a small problem. He named Stanford the champion before the team played Alabama in the Rose Bowl. The game ended in a tie, which made some people think that maybe Stanford wasn't the best team after all. The difficulty of crowning a champ before all the games were played would plague college football for decades.

The Dickinson System, as it came to be known, opened a floodgate. Soon other people developed their own systems, each proclaiming a national champion (and rarely agreeing with one another). Still, for a decade, the Dickinson System carried the most weight with fans. Its winner was, in the eyes of most, the true national champ.

Then, in 1936, Associated Press (AP) sports editor Alan J. Gould had a new idea about how to select a college football champion. Gould conducted a poll of sportswriters, asking them to rank the best teams from the previous season. His poll resulted in a three-way split for the 1935 title. Minnesota, Princeton, and Southern Methodist shared honors as the AP champs. (Minnesota was the champion, according to the Dickinson System). Gould polled the writers again after the 1936 season. This time, Minnesota stood alone as the national champion.

Other polls and other systems existed, which usually led to multiple teams claiming the national title. But by the 1940s, fans and schools generally accepted the AP poll as the measuring stick for deciding the best team in the land. Finally, it seemed that college football had settled on a method of determining a single, undisputed champion. And then at the beginning of the next decade, everything changed.

Football players in the early 1900s didn't wear as much protective gear as they do in the modern game.

A TALE OF TWO POLLS

In 1950 United Press International (UPI) was AP's main competitor among news organizations. UPI wasn't content to let AP gain all the credit and publicity for determining college football's champion. That year UPI began a poll of its own. It aimed to trump the AP by going to a source that many would consider more reliable than sportswriters: college football coaches.

College football fans try to stay dry at the Rose Bowl in January 1955.

The two-poll era had begun. At first, little changed. The AP and UPI polls both named Oklahoma the 1950 champs. They agreed on Tennessee in 1951, Michigan State in 1952, and Maryland in 1953.

The agreement ended in 1954. That season three teams posted perfect regular-season records. Ohio State and UCLA each went 9 – 0, while Oklahoma was 10 – 0. The final AP poll (conducted before the end-of-season bowl games) gave the Ohio State Buckeyes the No. 1 spot, while the UPI poll went with UCLA. Both polls had Oklahoma ranked third.

It was almost a perfect scenario. Normally, the champions of the Big Ten Conference, Ohio State, and the Pacific Coast Conference (PCC), UCLA, squared off in the Rose Bowl—in 1954 it would have been a true national championship game. But NCAA rules prohibited a team from playing in a bowl in consecutive years. UCLA had played in the Rose Bowl the previous year, so PCC runner-up USC went instead. And Oklahoma was prevented from playing in a bowl game because they'd played in the Orange Bowl a season before.

That left Ohio State as the only unbeaten team eligible to play in a postseason bowl in 1954. The Buckeyes staked their claim to the title with a 20 – 7 victory over USC in the Rose Bowl, but it made no difference in the final polls. The national championship was split between Ohio State and UCLA—and unbeaten Oklahoma didn't even share a piece of it. In the end, two disagreeing polls left three schools feeling dissatisfied.

The 1954 season was just the beginning of years of problems with the two-poll system. For the next four decades, the system would frustrate players, coaches, and fans alike. From 1951 to 1991, the AP and UPI polls produced split results nine times, including back-to-back seasons in 1990 and 1991.

COALITIONS AND ALLIANCES

The climate of college football had changed a lot by the 1990s. The sport had become a huge business, with schools and conferences raking in millions of dollars from ticket sales and television deals. And the biggest cash cow was bowl season. Fans loved the pageantry and drama of bowls, and the number of bowl games grew. In 1930 the Rose Bowl had been the only major college bowl game. By 1940 there were five bowls. By 1990 there were 19. Certain bowls were affiliated with certain conferences.

THE ROSE BOWL

Even most die-hard modern college football fans probably can't list every bowl game. There are dozens, and new bowls are frequently added. But it hasn't always been that way. At one time, the Rose Bowl in Pasadena, California, dubbed the granddaddy of them all, was the only bowl around.

The first Rose Bowl was played on January 1, 1902, as a way of raising money to stage the popular Rose Parade in Pasadena. The game was touted as an East vs. West affair, pitting California's Stanford against Michigan. It wasn't much of a game, however. Michigan completely destroyed the hapless Stanford team. With the score at 49–0 in the third quarter, Stanford had seen enough and left the field. Michigan had a perfect 11–0 record for the season and was hailed as the national champion.

The Rose Bowl remained college football's only major bowl until 1935, when the Sugar Bowl, Orange Bowl, and Sun Bowl were added. In the 1940s, the conferences that would become the Big Ten and the PCC agreed to send their champions to battle in the Rose Bowl each year. They came to the agreement in part because schools in both conferences favored racial integration in college athletics. Other powerful conferences, such as the SEC, wouldn't integrate until the 1960s.

The Rose Bowl, for example, usually featured a showdown between the champions of the Big Ten and Pacific-10 (Pac-10) conferences. Other bowls could invite any teams they pleased. And the top football programs often had their choice of bowl games. Add it all up, and a matchup between the nation's two top teams in a bowl game that would constitute a true national title game was rare.

The financial success of bowl games had made the NCAA reluctant to change its postseason structure. But after split titles in 1990 and 1991, fan outcry finally forced a change. In 1992 the major conferences and bowl games combined to form the Bowl Coalition. The coalition was designed to force a true title game, No. 1 vs. No. 2, and to end split championships. The new Bowl Poll combined the AP and UPI polls to determine the land's top two teams. They would then face off in a title game.

The system worked without a hitch in its first season. Second-ranked Alabama pulled off an upset of top-ranked Miami in the Sugar Bowl, 34–14. College football fans had an undisputed champion.

But cracks in the system began to show the following year. The 1993 season saw two teams—Nebraska and West Virginia—finish the regular season undefeated. Yet the Bowl Poll ranked Florida State, a team with one loss, ahead of West Virginia in its final rankings. The Florida State Seminoles went on to beat Nebraska in the Orange Bowl, 18–16, and win the national championship. It would have been a disaster for the Bowl Coalition if the Florida Gators hadn't trounced West Virginia in the Sugar Bowl, 41–7. If West Virginia had won, they would have been undefeated for the season, yet still ranked behind once-beaten Florida State.

A larger problem surfaced a year later. Nebraska won the Big Eight Conference and was the top-ranked team in the nation. Penn State of the Big Ten won their conference and finished the season ranked second. But the top two teams couldn't meet in a bowl game because the Big Ten and Pac-10 conferences were obligated to send their champions to the Rose Bowl. Penn State beat Oregon in the Rose Bowl while Nebraska beat No. 3 Florida State in the Orange Bowl. Penn State didn't lose a

Alabama coach Gene Stallings celebrates with his team after defeating Miami in the Sugar Bowl on January 1, 1993.

game all season, but it wasn't enough for a piece of the title, which went to Nebraska.

The Bowl Coalition was clearly flawed. In 1995 it was replaced by a new agreement called the Bowl Alliance. It made some changes to the way teams were chosen for bowl games, but at its heart, the system still relied on the AP and UPI polls. And the Bowl Alliance didn't address the main obstacle to a true national title game—the Rose Bowl's hold on the Big Ten and Pac-10 champs. Only one out of the next three seasons saw a title game featuring the nation's two top-ranked teams. Then, in 1997, the AP voters gave their title to Big Ten champ Michigan. The UPI poll, meanwhile, named Nebraska the champs. It was an embarrassment to college football that despite its best efforts to avoid split titles, the exact scenario had played out for the third time in eight years.

ENTER THE BCS

The Rose Bowl had been a major thorn in the side of the Bowl Alliance. That thorn was finally removed in 1998 with the introduction of the Bowl Championship Series (BCS). The BCS included all the major conferences and bowls—including the Rose Bowl, which was persuaded to release its hold on any Big Ten or Pac-10 champ that qualified for the title game—to ensure a true championship showdown. The nation's top two teams would face off in a bowl game, no matter which conference they came from. That season Tennessee became the first BCS champ by defeating Florida State in the Fiesta Bowl, 23–16.

Peerless Price *(left)* of the Tennessee Volunteers catches a pass against Florida State during the Fiesta Bowl.

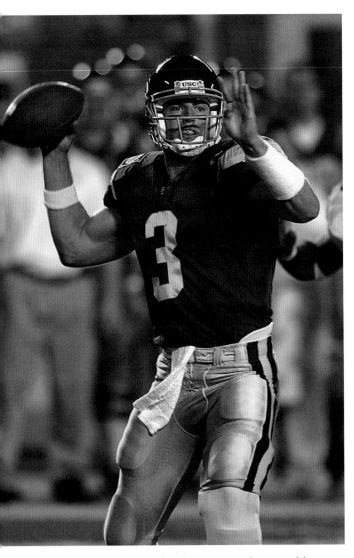

In 2003 USC quarterback Carson Palmer and his teammates lost only one game.

While the BCS eliminated one of the major problems that had plagued college football, it also created new problems. The BCS chose the top two teams using a complex combination of two polls and a computer ranking. The computer ranking factored in a team's record, the strength of its schedule, and other things. This system soon fell under scrutiny, in part because it also rewarded teams for positive point differentials in games. Teams hoping to secure a top place in the BCS rankings were all but forced to run up the score on inferior teams. This made for many lopsided games. In addition, teams that were not members of the six major conferences, with the lone exception of Notre Dame, were ineligible to play in the title game.

Fans hoped that the BCS would end split championships once and for all by including all the major conferences under one system. But it didn't. In 2003 no team finished the regular season unbeaten. But three—Oklahoma, LSU, and USC—finished with just a single loss. Both the AP and UPI polls ranked the USC Trojans as the top team in the land. But after combining the poll results with the mathematical formula, the final rankings matched Oklahoma and LSU in the Sugar Bowl for the championship game—leaving the No. 1 team in the AP and UPI polls out of the game altogether! LSU beat Oklahoma, while USC defeated fourth-ranked Michigan in the Rose Bowl.

The final UPI poll of the season honored the result of the official title game, naming LSU the national champion. But USC took the top spot in the final AP poll. Even with the BCS in place, college football couldn't escape the specter of a split championship. Fan and media outcry was intense. The BCS, which had already been unpopular with fans before the fiasco of 2003, became a punch line to many. Its reputation never fully recovered.

A NEW ERA

Fans all around the nation wanted a playoff system to determine the college football champion. Finally, in 2012, the NCAA relented. It announced a four-team playoff system beginning in the 2014 season. Each season a selection committee, made up of college athletic directors, former players and coaches, and other officials, would choose the four playoff teams. The teams would be determined by their records, the quality of their opponents, the results of head-to-head matchups, and other factors. None of the conferences or independent teams would be excluded from the playoff.

The new College Football Playoff was a success with fans, though it did not eliminate all controversy. Alabama, Florida State, and Oregon were consensus picks for the first playoff. But three teams—Ohio State, TCU, and Baylor—felt they had strong claims to the final spot. In the end, Ohio State was chosen for the playoff and then won back-to-back upsets over Alabama and Oregon to earn the first national championship of the new era. After more than a century of controversy and split titles, college football may have finally found a system that will crown a single, undisputed champ each season.

2 SETTLING IT ON THE FIELD
GREAT NATIONAL TITLE GAMES

Nothing in college football can compare to a true championship game, pitting the top two teams in the land in a battle for the title. The early years of college football provided few such games. But with the dawn of the BCS, fans have been treated to many championship thrills and heartaches. Here are just a few of history's most memorable college football title games.

THE FOOTBALL CHAMPIONSHIP OF AMERICA

University of Alabama vs. Stanford University

January 1, 1927

The buzz surrounding the 1927 Rose Bowl was unlike anything college football fans had ever seen. The nation's two best teams, the Stanford Cardinal and the Alabama Crimson Tide, were facing off in a game that the press dubbed the "Football Championship of America." Demand for tickets was so high that Rose Bowl officials added bleachers to seat an extra 4,000 fans. Many more people listened on the radio—it was the first college football game ever broadcast live to a nationwide audience.

The game started with a bang. On Stanford's first play, fullback Clifford Hoffman chucked a 40-yard pass to tight end Ted Shipkey. Stanford missed a field goal attempt a few plays later, but they had managed to establish critical field position by driving down the field. Later in the first quarter, Stanford punched it into the end zone on a 5-yard pass from George Bogue to Ed Walker.

The game remained 7 – 0 in favor of Stanford deep into the fourth quarter. Late in the final period, Alabama forced a Stanford punt. The Crimson Tide ran hard at the punter to try to block the kick. The strategy worked. Alabama's Baba Pearce batted the ball backward, and the Crimson Tide took possession of the ball at Stanford's 14-yard line.

Alabama finally had a great chance to put some points on the board. But Crimson Tide head coach Wallace Wade knew that his offense was tired. He inserted running back Jimmy Johnson into the game. Johnson, one of the team's best runners, was struggling with a dislocated shoulder and hadn't played all day. But he was the man who finally put Alabama on the board with a 1-yard scamper into the end zone. The score was 7 – 6 with little time remaining in the game. It all came down to the extra-point kick.

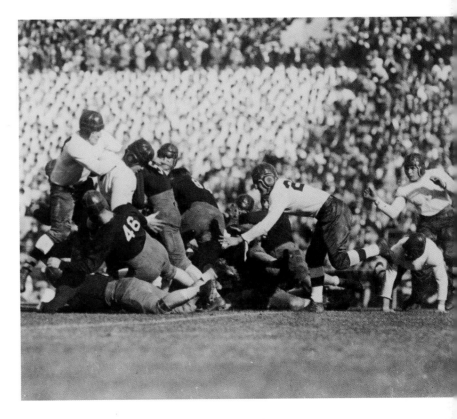

Players pile up during the 1927 Rose Bowl.

In the modern game, extra-point tries often feel like formalities. Kickers at the college level have only one job, and they rarely miss. But in 1927, teams didn't spend much time practicing extra points, and the players who performed them were not kicking specialists. That meant extra points were no sure thing. But Coach Wade had a trick up his sleeve to ensure that his kicker would have plenty of time to make the extra point. As the teams lined up for the kick, an Alabama player stood up and yelled, "Signals off!" The call confused the Stanford players, many of whom believed that Alabama was stopping the play. But the call was really the cue for the center to snap the ball. The Stanford defenders had little chance to rush kicker Herschel Caldwell, who calmly booted it through the uprights to tie the game, 7 – 7.

Stanford got the ball back at their own 22-yard line. But the team had time for only two plays before the game clock expired. With no overtime in college football at the time, the game ended in a tie. Alabama and Stanford shared the national title.

JUST SHORT

USC vs. the University of Wisconsin

January 1, 1963

At first, the 1963 Rose Bowl didn't look much like a classic. The No. 1-ranked USC Trojans were in complete control for most of the game. Trojan quarterback Pete Beathard marched his offense up and down the field, while the second-ranked Wisconsin Badgers struggled to maintain drives. After Beathard's fourth touchdown pass early in the fourth quarter, the Trojans had a huge lead, 42 – 14, and the Rose Bowl stands slowly began to empty of fans.

With a four-touchdown advantage, many of the Trojan players let down their guard. "Some of our guys were congratulating each other, like the game was over," said USC head coach John McKay. But there was still almost a full quarter of football to play.

Wisconsin running back Ralph Kurek *(left, in white)* scores a touchdown against USC on January 1, 1963.

Wisconsin quarterback Ron Vander Kelen wasn't ready to pack it in. In the game's final 14 minutes, he put on one of the most impressive passing displays in Rose Bowl history. And it happened fast. The Badgers scored on an 80-yard drive, then recovered a fumble on USC's first play of the next drive. Vander Kelen quickly struck again with another touchdown. Just like that, USC's lead had been trimmed to 14 points, 42–28. Soon after, the Trojans botched a snap while trying to punt from deep in their own end. The play led to a safety, making the score USC 42, Wisconsin 30.

The wheels were coming off for USC as time ran out on the Rose Bowl. The safety forced USC to kick the ball back to the Badgers. Vander Kelen drove Wisconsin down the field. With 1:19 to play in the game, he connected with Pat Richter on a 19-yard touchdown pass to make the score 42–37.

It was a dizzying comeback attempt. USC's 28-point lead had been cut to five. But the Badgers fell just short. Wisconsin attempted an onside kick, hoping to get the ball back for one last chance to score. But USC covered the ball and managed to kill the clock to preserve the victory. In the end, the USC lead had indeed been too large to overcome. But what had started out as a yawner turned into one of the most thrilling national title game finishes of all time.

DOMINATING IN DEFEAT

Penn State University vs. the University of Miami

January 1, 1987

The 1987 Fiesta Bowl was supposed to be a lopsided affair. The top-ranked Miami Hurricanes had been the college football equivalent of a freight train all season long, going undefeated and outscoring opponents 420–136. Heisman Trophy-winning quarterback Vinny Testaverde led a team packed with future NFL stars. The second-ranked Penn State Nittany Lions were also undefeated. But their season had been marked by a series of close calls—many of them against marginal competition. Few gave the workmanlike Nittany Lions much chance of weathering the Hurricanes.

The action on the field seemed to validate that viewpoint. Miami dominated the slower, less-talented Nittany Lions. Testaverde and the Hurricane offense gained 445 yards in the game compared to just 162 yards for Penn State. The Hurricanes had 22 first downs to Penn State's meager eight. By almost every measurable statistic, the Hurricanes utterly had their way with Penn State.

One statistic, however, kept Penn State in the game. Despite driving up and down the field at will, Testaverde and the Hurricanes were plagued by turnovers. And so, despite their complete domination in yards gained and first downs, Miami led by a mere three points in the fourth quarter.

With less than nine minutes to play in the game, Testaverde took a snap, dropped back, and whipped a pass down the field. Penn State linebacker Shane Conlan, playing on an injured leg, stepped in front of the pass for an interception. Conlan hustled 40 yards down the field before being tackled at Miami's 5-yard line. Penn State running back D. J. Dozier finished the job with a touchdown run to give the Nittany Lions a shocking 14–10 lead.

Miami still had plenty of time. They needed a touchdown to take the lead. Testaverde marched the Hurricanes all the way to the opposing goal line. But Penn State stepped up. They sacked Testaverde and eventually forced a winner-take-all, fourth-and-goal play with 18 seconds remaining. Testaverde zipped a pass into the end zone. The Nittany Lions linebacker Pete Giftopoulos picked it off, preventing Miami from scoring and sealing one of the most improbable national championships in college football history.

DOUBLE THE FUN

University of Miami vs. Ohio State University
January 3, 2003

In 2002 the Miami Hurricanes were building a dynasty. They were the defending national champions and had surged to a perfect 12 – 0 record in the regular season. Few expected the second-ranked Ohio State Buckeyes to have much chance of slowing down Miami's high-powered offense in the Fiesta Bowl. Yet it was the Ohio State defense that dominated the first half, forcing Miami to turn the ball over and giving the underdog Buckeyes a halftime lead, 14 – 7. Early in the third quarter, Ohio State extended that lead to 17 – 7 with a field goal. Miami was ready with an answer. Running back Willis McGahee powered the Hurricanes down the field and punched the ball into the end zone to make the score 17 – 14.

Willis McGahee scores for Miami.

The fourth quarter was a defensive slugfest. Neither team could sustain a long drive. With the score still 17 – 14 in Ohio State's advantage and a little more than two minutes to go, the Buckeyes were forced to punt. The Hurricanes had one last chance to tie or win the game. Miami punt returner Roscoe Parrish fielded the punt at his own 25-yard line. Parrish then sliced through the Buckeye coverage team, streaking 50 yards and giving Miami great field position. The Hurricanes kicked a game-tying field goal on the final play of the fourth quarter. Overtime!

For overtime the teams would take turns possessing the ball, each starting on the opposing team's 25-yard line. The Hurricanes wasted little time scoring on the opening possession. Quarterback Ken Dorsey threaded a touchdown pass over the middle to big tight end Kellen Winslow.

Ohio State needed a touchdown to stay alive. A penalty and a sack left the Buckeyes facing fourth down and 14 yards to go from the 29-yard line. But their dim hopes grew brighter when quarterback Craig Krenzel flipped a pass to Michael Jenkins for 17 yards to keep the drive alive.

Three plays later, the Buckeyes faced another fourth down. Krenzel dropped back and lofted a pass toward the back corner of the end zone. Receiver Chris Gamble reached up for the ball, but it glanced off his fingers and fell incomplete. The celebration was on for Miami fans and players—two straight national titles!

But the celebration was short-lived. One of the referees had hurled his yellow flag in the air. It was a pass interference penalty against Miami. The Hurricanes were irate at what appeared to be a questionable call. Three plays later, Krenzel punched it in to tie the game. Double overtime!

In the second overtime, Ohio State started with the ball. This time, they kept it on the ground and steamrolled Miami's defense. On the fifth play of the drive, running back Maurice Clarett plunged five yards up the middle for the go-ahead touchdown.

Miami took over. They moved the ball all the way to the Ohio State 2-yard line. That's when the Buckeye defense stepped up with one of the great goal-line stands of all time. On first down, Miami running back Jarrett Payton managed just one yard. Dorsey's pass on second down fell incomplete. On third down, the swarming Ohio State defense stuffed running back Quadtrine Hill for no gain. Miami elected to pass on fourth down. But Ohio State pass rushers got to Dorsey. From the clutches of a defender, Dorsey launched a desperation pass into the end zone. It fell harmlessly to the ground. The game was over. The Buckeyes had won one of the most exciting— and most controversial—national title games ever.

Ohio State storms the field in celebration after beating Miami in the 2003 Fiesta Bowl.

THE GREATEST?

University of Texas vs. USC

January 4, 2006

The 2006 Rose Bowl featured a matchup for the ages. The No. 1-ranked Trojans were riding a 34-game winning streak and were the defending national champs. The second-ranked Texas Longhorns had won 19 straight games. Both teams were packed

with NFL-caliber stars. Just weeks before the game, USC running back Reggie Bush had edged Texas quarterback Vince Young for the Heisman Trophy.

The Rose Bowl was a thrilling back-and-forth slugfest, with two seemingly unstoppable offenses trading blows. USC quarterback Matt Leinart lit up the Texas defense with pinpoint passes. Young did much of his damage with his legs, scrambling and darting through the Trojan defense.

With just over eight minutes to go in the fourth quarter, USC led by five, 31–26. They also had possession of the ball. Leinart was at his best, ripping off one big play after another. It took him less than two minutes to lead the Trojans down the field. USC capped off the drive when Leinart found

Quarterback Vince Young gets fired up before the start of the 2006 Rose Bowl.

receiver Dwayne Jarrett open and hit him with a pass. Texas cornerback Tarell Brown slammed violently into Jarrett, but Brown couldn't bring the USC receiver down in time. Jarrett stretched the ball over the goal line for a touchdown. The Trojans improved their lead to 12 points, 38–26.

It was a big lead for USC. But the Jarrett touchdown may have come too quickly. A lot of time was still left in the game. Young and the Longhorns drove the ball down the field. Then the big quarterback scampered 17 yards into the end zone to cut the lead to five points, 38–33.

USC took possession of the ball and tried to run time off the clock. But they soon faced a fourth down with two yards to go on the Texas 45-yard line. Fewer than three minutes remained in the game. USC head coach Pete Carroll could have elected to punt the ball. That would have forced the Longhorns to put together a long drive to score a touchdown. Instead, Carroll elected to go for the first down. Leinart handed the ball off to big, bruising running back LenDale White. The Texas defense was ready. They swarmed White and brought him down short of the first-down marker. Texas ball!

Young had been great all day. But he was at his best as he calmly led the Longhorns' offense down the field to the USC 8-yard line. Just 26 seconds remained on the clock as Texas lined up in the shotgun formation. It was fourth down and five. The crowd was electric, knowing that this play could decide the national championship. Young took the snap and scanned the field. But he couldn't find an open receiver. That might have been a problem for most quarterbacks, but not for the fleet-footed Young. He broke out of the pocket and darted to the right. USC defenders desperately tried to rally to the ball, but Young was too quick. He sprinted into the corner of the end zone untouched.

The Longhorns pushed their lead to 41–38 with a two-point conversion. When the Trojans couldn't create a miracle in the final seconds, the game was over. The high-scoring battle was, in the eyes of many, the greatest title game of all time.

GRAND FINALE

Florida State University vs. Auburn University

January 6, 2014

The BCS may have been the target of constant criticism during its time, but it went out with a bang. The 2014 Rose Bowl battle between top-ranked Florida State and No. 2 Auburn, which marked the final game played under the BCS system, was one for the ages.

The unbeaten Florida State Seminoles were heavy favorites entering the game. Quarterback Jameis Winston, who that season had become just the second freshman ever to win the Heisman Trophy, had led his team to a dominant record and the top ranking. Yet for many, the more interesting story was that of the Auburn Tigers, perhaps the least likely BCS title game entrant in history. Just a year earlier, Auburn had struggled through a miserable 3–9 season. But under first-year coach Gus Malzahn,

they bounced back in a big way. The Tigers tore through the ultracompetitive SEC and crowned the regular season with a thrilling, last-second victory over Alabama, the nation's top-ranked team at the time. Fans and reporters, captivated by the idea of such a monumental turnaround in the span of a single season, dubbed Auburn a team of destiny.

Auburn lived up to that billing in the first three quarters against Florida State. The Tigers' speedy, cunning defense stifled the Seminoles' air attack. Winston struggled to find open receivers. Meanwhile, Auburn quarterback Nick Marshall threw for two touchdowns and ran for a third. After three quarters, the Tigers led, 21–13.

The close score set up an epic fourth quarter with the national title on the line. Auburn had the ball early in the quarter with a chance to take a two-score lead. But Florida State cornerback

P. J. Williams picked off a Marshall pass to give the Seminoles great field position. Winston wasted little time in capitalizing on Auburn's mistake. He flipped an 11-yard touchdown pass to fullback Chad Abram to cut Auburn's lead to a single point, 21–20.

Auburn answered with a long, grinding drive that took almost seven minutes off the game clock. They drove the ball all the way to Florida State's 6-yard line. But Marshall's pass on third down and four fell incomplete, forcing the Tigers to settle for a field goal. The score was Auburn 24, Florida State 20.

Auburn fans had little time to savor their four-point lead. Florida State's Kermit Whitfield fielded Auburn's kickoff at his own goal line. Whitfield sprinted forward through a gulf opened by Florida State's blockers. He cut toward the left sideline and turned on the jets. The crowd roared as Whitfield pulled away and burned 100 yards for the go-ahead score.

On the ensuing possession, Marshall led Auburn back down the field. With just 90 seconds to go in the game, the Tigers faced second down and 16. Marshall took the snap and handed off to running back Tre Mason. Mason darted right, ducked past one tackler, bowled over another, and carried the ball 37 yards for a thrilling touchdown. With a 31–27 lead, Auburn once again looked like a team of destiny.

Winston and the Seminoles took possession of the ball at their own 20-yard line with just one minute, 11 seconds remaining. The Heisman winner led his team on one of the most dramatic drives in college football history. On the second play, he hit Rashad Greene with a pass over the middle. The receiver blasted through two tacklers and darted 49 yards down the field.

The Seminoles continued to march. With just 17 seconds to go, they had the ball on Auburn's 2-yard line. Winston took the snap, faked a handoff, and fired a high pass into the middle of the end zone. Receiver Kelvin Benjamin used all of his six-foot-five frame to reach and snatch the ball out of the air. Touchdown! The Seminoles had completed their perfect season and helped make the final BCS title game a memorable one.

3 BUILDING A LEGEND
DYNASTIES OF COLLEGE FOOTBALL

Dozens of universities have claimed one or more national championships. But only a select few schools have accomplished the ultimate in the sport—a true dynasty of dominance over a period of years. Because athletes usually only play with a school for three or four years, building a core that can win consistently from season to season is the biggest challenge for a coach and an athletic program. It takes great coaching, talented players, and even a little bit of luck.

EARLY DYNASTIES

Dynasties in college football are nothing new. They stretch as far back as the sport itself. Yale created one of the first college football dynasties. This Ivy League school was one of a handful of universities that dominated college football in the late 1800s. And while many of those early programs faded as the game spread across the country, Yale remained near the top. From 1905 through 1909, the Yale Bulldogs were all but unbeatable. It started with a 1905 season that saw Yale go 10 – 0 and outscore their opponents by a combined score of 227 – 4. Over that five-year period, the Bulldogs only lost one game!

And 20 years later, Howard Jones—the head coach of the 1909 Yale football team—went on to build another dynasty on the other side of the country. Jones led USC to at least a share of the national title in 1928, 1929, 1931, 1932, and 1933.

In 1934 coach Bernie Bierman and the Minnesota Golden Gophers were ready to take over the mantle of top team in the land. The Gophers went 8 – 0 in 1934 to earn a share of the national title. They went 8 – 0 again in 1935 and were named co-champs in the very first AP college football poll. And then in 1936, a 7 – 1 record earned Minnesota sole honors as the AP champ and marked the end of their dynasty.

Coach Bierman (right) of the Golden Gophers led his team to the national title in 1934, 1935, and 1936.

UNIVERSITY OF NOTRE DAME (1946 – 1949)

The Notre Dame Fighting Irish had emerged as a top college football powerhouse in the 1920s. But it wasn't until 1946 that they began to build their first dynasty as the best team in the sport. Frank Leahy had taken over as Notre Dame's head coach in 1941 and had led the team to a championship in 1943. But Leahy had missed all the 1944 and 1945 seasons to fight for the United States in World War II (1939 – 1945). The Fighting Irish went 15 – 4 – 1 in his absence—a respectable, but not remarkable,

OFF TO WAR

Like many college football programs, Notre Dame lost players and coaches to World War II. Countless US athletes, like their fellow countrymen from all walks of life, left their regular lives behind to serve their country in the war.

One athlete-turned-soldier was Notre Dame quarterback and defensive back Johnny Lujack. Lujack left the university after his sophomore season to join the US Navy. He spent two years hunting enemy submarines before returning to the United States and to Notre Dame. Lujack was back on the gridiron in 1946 and led the Fighting Irish to the national title that year, as well as in 1947.

The Notre Dame football team meets on the field in 1947.

record. He returned in 1946, and the program instantly returned to the top.

The Notre Dame dynasty began with payback. Army was the top college team at the time. They had embarrassed Notre Dame in each of the past two seasons. When the teams met in 1946, Notre Dame players were eager for revenge. And they got it . . . kind of.

With the game scoreless in the third quarter, Army's star running back, Doc Blanchard, got loose in the open field. That could have been a recipe for disaster for Notre Dame. But Johnny Lujack—a quarterback who also played defensive back for the Irish—made an amazing tackle to prevent Blanchard from scoring. The game ended in a tie, 0 – 0. Neither Notre Dame nor Army lost a game that season, but the AP voters gave the 1946 national title to the Irish.

Johnny Lujack

Notre Dame repeated as champions in 1947, though again in a controversial manner. The Fighting Irish entered their final regular season game, against USC, ranked No. 2 in the nation. Michigan was No. 1 and had already completed its regular season. Notre Dame did its job, beating the Trojans in California, 38 – 7. That convinced the AP voters to give the Irish the top spot and the national title. However, at the time, the final vote came before the bowl games. Notre Dame wasn't eligible for a bowl game that season. When Michigan later trounced USC in the Rose Bowl, 49 – 0, it was clear to many that the title should have gone to the Wolverines.

USC was also instrumental in Notre Dame's title hopes in 1948. Once again, the teams met in the final game of the season. This time, the Trojans played the Irish to a 14 – 14 tie. This opened the door for Michigan to take the national title and a measure of revenge. In 1949 the Irish completed a perfect 10 – 0 season with their third title in four years. From 1946 to 1949, Notre Dame didn't lose a single game. Even more amazing, they never trailed a game at any point!

UNIVERSITY OF OKLAHOMA (1953 – 1957)

Strict, stern head coach Bud Wilkinson—a quarterback and lineman on Minnesota's dynasty of the 1930s—helped build another dynasty with the Oklahoma Sooners in the 1950s. Unlike some major college coaches, Wilkinson didn't comb the nation for the top players. He preferred to recruit local boys. He went on to prove that building a dynasty wasn't just about acquiring the top talent. It was about coaching and teamwork.

At first, the 1953 season didn't seem like the start of something big. The Sooners lost their first game to Notre Dame and then played to a tie with Pittsburgh in Oklahoma's second game. Finally, in their third contest, the Sooners scored a 19 – 14 victory over rival Texas. It was the beginning of one of the greatest streaks in college football history. Including the win against Texas, the Sooners would go on to win 47 straight games.

The Sooners knocked off top-ranked Maryland in the Orange Bowl that season. Before the game, Wilkinson created a fake playbook. Then he left it where he knew Maryland coaches would find it. The tactic worked. Maryland couldn't predict the plays the Sooners would call, and Oklahoma earned the victory. But because the AP poll was conducted before the game, Maryland was voted the official champion.

The Sooners were denied a championship again in 1954 despite a perfect 10 – 0 record. AP voters ranked them third, behind Ohio State and UCLA. But spotless marks in 1955 and 1956 each resulted in national championships. Oklahoma's 47-game winning streak came to an end early in the 1957 season in a loss to Notre Dame. But the Sooners' place as one of college football's greatest dynasties was set.

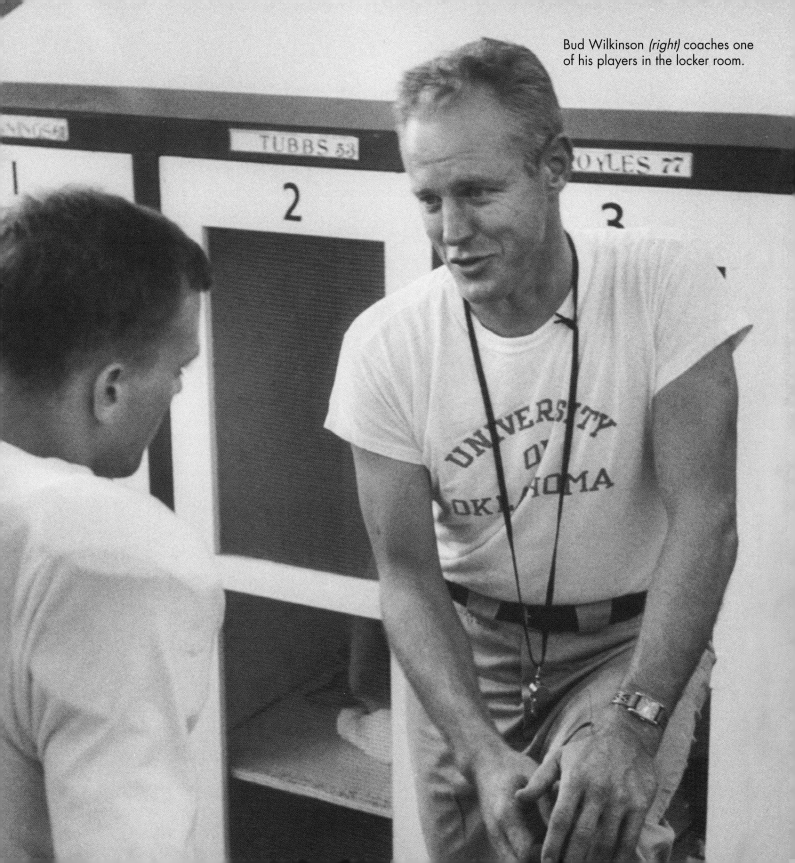

Bud Wilkinson *(right)* coaches one of his players in the locker room.

UNIVERSITY OF ALABAMA (1961–1966)

In the late 1950s, Alabama was far from a dynasty. In fact, they were a laughingstock of college football. In 1955 the team hit rock bottom, going 0–10 for the season. Alabama was desperate for a change. In 1958 they lured former Crimson Tide player Paul "Bear" Bryant away from Texas A&M to take over as head coach.

Bryant turned the program around—in a big way. By 1961 the team was a true force. Its signature was its stifling defense, led by tackling machine Lee Roy Jordan. Some have called the 1961 Alabama defense the greatest in the history of the sport. They never gave up more than seven points in a game. And in their final five games, they didn't allow a single point. They won those games by a combined score of 151–0! The Crimson Tide capped the championship season with a victory over Arkansas in the Sugar Bowl.

In 1962 the Tide stood at 8–0 with hopes of repeating as champions. In a November game against Georgia Tech, Alabama scored a touchdown to pull within a point, 7–6. There wasn't much time left in the game. Bryant feared that a tie would cost his team a shot at the title. So

Coach Paul "Bear" Bryant *(right)* helped turn Alabama into a powerhouse in the 1960s.

he went for a two-point conversion. Bryant pulled star quarterback Joe Namath from the game and inserted backup Jack Hurlbut, who was a better runner. The Georgia Tech defense knew what was coming, and they were ready. They stuffed Hurlbut short of the end zone, ending Alabama's hopes of a repeat championship.

Two years later, Alabama managed another perfect 10 – 0 regular season and were ranked No. 1. But they were far from the dominant team they'd been in 1961. This time many of their victories had been tight games. Yet the AP voters awarded them the national title—before the bowl games. The Tide went on to lose the Orange Bowl to Texas, while second-ranked Arkansas won the Cotton Bowl. Still, because of the timing of the final poll, Alabama was the national champ. It was the final straw for the AP. Beginning the following season, the final AP poll was conducted after the bowl games, in large part because of what fans called a fraudulent Alabama championship in 1964.

The 1965 Crimson Tide weren't given much chance to repeat, with stars such as quarterback Joe Namath having moved on to pro ball. After the Tide lost their opening game, any notion of a championship seemed a fantasy. Alabama recovered, however, winning or tying their remaining regular season games and climbing to the fourth spot in the AP poll. That set up one of the wildest days in college football history. Top-ranked Michigan State lost the Rose Bowl, and then No. 2 Arkansas lost the Cotton Bowl. Just like that, the Orange Bowl duel between the third-ranked Nebraska Cornhuskers and fourth-ranked Crimson Tide was for the championship! The Tide seized the opportunity, defeating the Cornhuskers, 39 – 28. With all the nation's top three teams losing, Alabama had earned one of the most unlikely championships in college football history—their third in five years.

The dynasty ended, strangely, with a perfect 1966 season. Alabama entered the season ranked No. 1, and the Tide won all of their games. Yet by season's end, the Tide ranked third, behind Notre Dame and Michigan State, both with records of 9 – 0 – 1. Some argued that Notre Dame and Michigan State had played tougher schedules. Others believed that the final ranking was politically motivated. Alabama was one of the few college football programs that was still not racially integrated. The team had only white players, and some AP voters may have tried to send Alabama a message by ranking them behind Notre Dame and Michigan State. It would be five more seasons before the Tide welcomed their first black player.

UNIVERSITY OF NEBRASKA (1993–1997)

The dominant team of the mid-1990s was the Nebraska Cornhuskers, known to fans as Big Red. The dynasty started with a near championship and ended with a split championship, with two undisputed titles in between.

After the 1993 season, the No. 2-ranked Cornhuskers met top-ranked Florida State in the Orange Bowl. The battle of unbeaten teams lived up to the hype. Florida State clung to a two-point lead in the final seconds, 18–16. Nebraska had time for one last play—a 45-yard field goal attempt. But the kick sailed left. Florida State was the champ.

Nebraska head coach Tom Osborne and his team wouldn't have to wait long for redemption. Big Red came into the 1994 season with something to prove, evidenced by their team slogan, Unfinished Business. It was not idle talk. The Huskers were utterly dominant, led by star quarterback "Touchdown" Tommie Frazier. The Huskers powered their way to the top ranking and a date with the Miami Hurricanes at the Orange Bowl. The Hurricanes jumped out to an early 17–7 lead, but Nebraska regained control, using their superior size and physical play to wear down Miami. Nebraska defensive back Kareem Moss intercepted a Miami pass late in the game to seal the win, 24–17. The celebration was on for Nebraska and its fans.

As good as the 1994 Cornhuskers were, the 1995 version was better. Frazier and the Nebraska offense were unstoppable, averaging 53 points per game for the season. None of their games were even close as the team went undefeated.

Nebraska met the unbeaten Florida Gators in the Fiesta Bowl, and the Huskers left no doubt about who deserved the No. 1 ranking. They rolled over Florida's defense

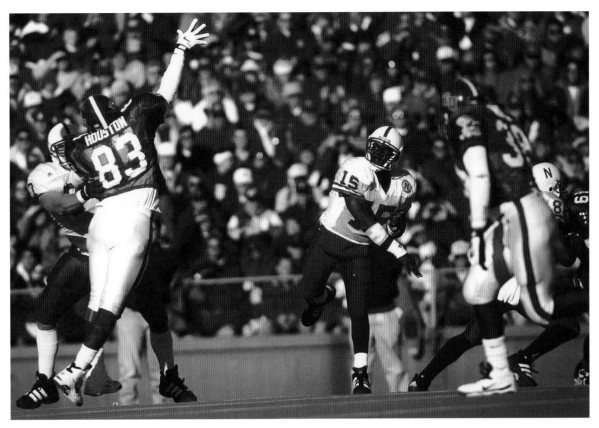

Nebraska's Tommie Frazier *(center)* hurls a deep pass during the 1994 season.

time and again, moving it up and down the field at will. Nebraska rushed the ball for a jaw-dropping 524 yards in the game. By contrast, the Florida rushing game lost 28 yards! The final score of 62 – 24 was one of the most lopsided in the history of college football championship games and left some fans asking whether the 1995 Cornhuskers were the greatest college football team in history.

With Frazier and other key players leaving school after the 1995 championship, the Cornhuskers took a small step back in 1996 with a record of 11 – 2. But they were right back in the championship mix in 1997—Osborne's final season as head coach. Nebraska and Michigan—both undefeated for the season—dueled for the top ranking. The voters gave the first spot to Michigan, with the bowls yet to play.

Michigan beat Washington State in the Rose Bowl, while second-ranked Nebraska crushed No. 3 Tennessee, 42 – 17, in the Orange Bowl.

The blowout win over Tennessee was enough to convince UPI voters that Nebraska was the top team in the land. But the AP voters disagreed, giving the honor to Michigan. The controversial split championship helped give rise to the BCS, which debuted the following season. In the final tally, Nebraska earned at least a share of the national title in three out of four seasons, making Big Red of the mid-1990s a true dynasty.

UNIVERSITY OF ALABAMA (2009 – 2012)

The Crimson Tide remained a fixture near the top of the college football rankings for several decades after their dynasty of the 1960s. But by the mid-2000s, their legend had begun to fade. Since their 1992 national title, the Tide had cracked the top five in the AP's final poll just once. In 2007 the university lured Miami Dolphins coach Nick Saban away from the NFL to take over the once-storied program in Alabama.

Saban quickly restored the Crimson Tide's former glory. The team's record improved from 7 – 6 in 2007 to 12 – 2 in 2008. Then, in 2009, they took another giant step forward. Alabama went undefeated in the regular season to earn the No. 1 ranking and a BCS title bout with the No. 2 Texas Longhorns in the Rose Bowl.

The Texas defense stifled the Tide offense on the first drive. The Longhorns took over and began to march down the field. On the fifth play of the drive, Alabama lineman Marcell Dareus slammed into Colt McCoy, Texas's star quarterback. McCoy went to the ground in pain. He never returned to the game. The Tide controlled the ball with a powerful running attack led by freshman Trent Richardson, while the Longhorns' offense floundered without McCoy. The Tide led by 18 points at halftime and never looked back.

After putting up a mediocre 10 – 3 record in 2010, Saban and Alabama were back strong in 2011. Led by bruising running back Richardson and a swarming defense, the Tide entered the season ranked second in the nation and never dropped lower than No. 4, despite an overtime loss to the LSU Tigers, 9 – 6.

The Tigers went on to an undefeated season and the top ranking, while Alabama finished ranked No. 2, just beating out Oklahoma State. That set up a rematch of the season's top two teams, a rarity in college football. LSU may have gotten the best of the Tide in their first meeting that year. But the national championship game was all Alabama. The Tigers offense looked lost against the speedy Alabama

Trent Richardson (right) runs past LSU defenders.

Notre Dame quarterback Everett Golson *(right)* tries to evade an Alabama defender on January 8, 2013.

defense. LSU managed to advance the ball past the 50-yard line just once all game. Five field goals and a Trent Richardson touchdown gave the Tide a convincing 21–0 victory and their second title in three years.

The 2012 Crimson Tide season mirrored the 2011 campaign. Saban and the Tide overcame a single regular-season loss—this time to 15th-ranked Texas A&M—to win their conference and the second spot in the national rankings. In the BCS title game, Alabama dismantled the previously unbeaten and top-ranked Notre Dame Fighting Irish. The Tide took control early, building a 28-point lead by halftime, and rolled to victory. When the Gatorade bucket was dumped on Nick Saban in celebration of the championship for the third time in four years, Alabama's most recent dynasty was assured.

POLL CHAMPIONSHIPS

Since the college football poll era began in 1936, 30 schools have earned at least a share of the national title. Here they are, along with how many championships they have won:

University of Alabama	10		Michigan State University	2
Notre Dame University	8		Penn State University	2
University of Oklahoma	7		University of Pittsburgh	2
USC	7		University of Tennessee	2
Ohio State University	6		Brigham Young University	1
University of Miami	5		Clemson University	1
University of Nebraska	5		University of Colorado	1
University of Minnesota	4		University of Georgia	1
University of Texas	4		Georgia Tech	1
University of Florida	3		University of Maryland	1
Florida State University	3		Syracuse University	1
LSU	3		Texas Christian University	1
Army	2		Texas A&M University	1
Auburn University	2		UCLA	1
University of Michigan	2		University of Washington	1

4 UNFORGETTABLE
MEMORABLE MOMENTS OF THE
NATIONAL CHAMPIONSHIP

It's not always the dramatic finish or the big upset that makes a national championship game memorable. Sometimes, it's a single play, an amazing individual feat, a controversial referee call, or a coaching decision that has fans talking the next day and for years to come. From the embarrassing to the inspiring to the unbelievable, here are some of the most memorable moments in the history of the college football national championship.

ROY "WRONG-WAY" RIEGELS

Georgia Tech vs. the University of California, Berkeley (Cal)
1929

The 1929 Rose Bowl wasn't a true national title game. At the time, bowl matchups between the nation's two top-ranked teams were exceedingly rare. But the undefeated and No. 1-ranked Georgia Tech Yellow Jackets were indeed playing for a championship in 1929. A victory over the Cal Golden Bears would be the final feather in Georgia Tech's caps for the national title.

Opposite page: Roy Riegels *(left)* rushes the ball down the field—in the wrong direction.

It was a tight, defensive game. There was no score in the second quarter when Georgia Tech's Jack "Stumpy" Thomason fumbled the ball. Cal lineman Roy Riegels picked it up and started to run. Then Riegels turned 180 degrees and started to run in the other direction. He was going the wrong way! A Cal player caught up to Riegels and stopped him just before he crossed into his own end zone. Georgia Tech players arrived moments later, tackling Riegels at the 1-yard line. Cal elected to punt the ball rather than run a risky play from the goal line. But Georgia Tech blocked the kick for a safety.

Riegels blocked a Georgia Tech punt in the second half, and Cal kept the game close. But in the end, his wrong-way run and the two-point safety that followed were the difference in the game. Georgia Tech won, 8 – 7, a victory that earned them the national title.

FOURTH AND A FOOT

Penn State vs. the University of Alabama
1979

In 1979 the Sugar Bowl between No. 1 Penn State and No. 2 Alabama came down to a single play. Trailing by seven points late in the fourth quarter, Penn State faced fourth-and-goal from the 1-foot mark. The game and the national championship were on the line.

It had been a thrilling sequence of events to get the game to this dramatic point. Just two plays before, on second down, Penn State receiver Scott Fitzkee was about to score when Alabama defensive back Don McNeal freed himself from a block and drove Fitzkee out of bounds at the 1-yard line. Then, on third down, running back Matt Suhey tried to blast through the middle to the end zone. Finding no running lane, Suhey attempted to dive over the pile. A wall of defenders met him, denying him the touchdown.

Penn State quarterback Chuck Fusina asked how far the ball was from the goal line. "Bout a foot," answered Alabama linebacker Marty Lyons. "You better pass."

Penn State ignored Lyons's advice. On fourth down, Fusina handed off to running back Mike Guman. Guman never had a chance. The Alabama defense blasted through the Penn State line and brought him down short of the goal. It was the last shot Penn State would get. Alabama held on for the victory and the championship.

NO GUTS, NO GLORY

University of Nebraska vs. the University of Miami

1984

The 1984 Orange Bowl didn't feature the two top teams in the land, but the national championship was on the line anyway. Top-ranked Nebraska faced fifth-ranked Miami. In bowl games played earlier, the nation's second- and fourth-ranked teams had each lost their games, while No. 3 Auburn had escaped with an unimpressive victory in their bowl game, 9 – 7. That meant that Miami and Nebraska controlled their own destinies. A victory over the powerful Cornhuskers in the Orange Bowl would ensure the national championship for the Hurricanes. Likewise, a victory for Nebraska would give the Cornhuskers the title.

The Huskers were heavy favorites, but the Hurricanes stormed out to a 17 – 0 lead in the first quarter. Nebraska was desperate to put points on the board. They used a trick play called the fumblerooski, in which quarterback Turner Gill intentionally fumbled the ball and then faked a handoff to the running back. The Miami defense was confused. They realized too late that Nebraska offensive lineman Dean Steinkuhler had scooped up the ball and was rumbling down the field. Steinkuhler sneaked into the end zone for a 19-yard touchdown. The trick play—illegal in the modern game—got Nebraska back into the game.

With less than a minute to play in the fourth quarter, Nebraska trailed by seven points and faced a fourth down and eight from the Miami 24-yard line. Gill took the snap and ran to the right. He turned the corner and started up the field. As defenders

But referee John Soffey rushed to restore order. The game was not over, Soffey explained. One second had remained on the clock when Bell was tackled. That meant Nebraska had time for one more play.

Nebraska coach Tom Osborne sent kicker Byron Bennett in to attempt a game-winning 45-yard field goal. The snap and the hold were clean, and Bennett booted the ball over onrushing Florida State defenders. But it was no storybook ending for the Cornhuskers. Bennett hooked the kick badly to the left, and for the third time, the celebration was on for Florida State—this time for good.

CLARETT STRIPS IT

Ohio State vs. the University of Miami
2003

The 2003 Fiesta Bowl between top-ranked Miami and No. 2 Ohio State was a game for the ages, with one big play after another. But for many fans, the lasting memory of the game came on an amazing defensive play—by an offensive player!

In the third quarter, Ohio State was facing third-and-goal from the 6-yard line. Already leading, 14 – 7, the Buckeyes were looking to seize control of the game. That's when Miami linebacker Sean Taylor stepped in front of a poorly thrown Ohio State pass in the end zone for a potentially game-changing interception.

Taylor was off to the races in the other direction. He darted to the Miami 28-yard line, where Ohio State running back Maurice Clarett chased him down. But instead of tackling Taylor, Clarett reached out, grabbed the ball with both hands, and ripped it clean out of Taylor's grasp. Ohio State got the ball back with a fresh set of downs and managed a field goal to extend its lead. The Buckeyes won the game and the national championship in double overtime, 31 – 24. Without Clarett's incredible hustle, Ohio State's dramatic victory might never have happened.

Maurice Clarett punches the ball into the end zone during the 2003 Fiesta Bowl.

GINN TAKES IT TO THE HOUSE

Ohio State vs. the University of Florida

2007

Ohio State fans were excited to watch their No. 1-ranked Buckeyes take on the second-ranked Florida Gators in the 2007 BCS National Championship Game. That excitement reached a fevered pitch when kick returner Ted Ginn Jr. fielded the game's opening kickoff at his own 7-yard line. Ginn started carefully up the field, letting his teammates set up blocks in front of him. Then, when he saw daylight, he pounced. Ginn broke through the middle of the field, darted right, and streaked 93 yards down

Ted Ginn Jr. speeds down the sideline for a touchdown during the first play of the 2007 national title game.

the sideline and into the end zone. With the extra point, the Buckeyes had a 7 – 0 lead just 16 seconds into the game!

The return was the high point of the game for the Buckeyes, however. As Ginn and his teammates enthusiastically celebrated the huge play, the star wide receiver injured his foot. He limped back to the locker room and never returned to the field.

Without its most dynamic playmaker, the Ohio State offense appeared helpless. Star quarterback Troy Smith was limited to an embarrassing 35 yards passing while taking five sacks. Meanwhile, Florida quarterback Tim Tebow and his Gators teammates picked the Buckeyes apart. By the time it was over, Florida had a staggering 41– 14 victory, and Ginn's thrilling kickoff return seemed a distant memory.

JUST KEEP RUNNING

University of Oregon vs. Auburn University
2011

Oregon and Auburn were tied, 19 – 19, with just over two minutes remaining in the 2011 national title game. From his team's 40-yard line, freshman Auburn running back Michael Dyer took the handoff and ran to the right. Oregon safety Eddie Pleasant darted across the field, grabbed Dyer, and pulled him toward the ground.

Dyer rolled over Pleasant and onto his feet. Most people thought Dyer was down and the play was over. The players on the field stopped—including Dyer. But the referees didn't blow their whistles to end the play. Dyer realized that his knee had never actually touched the ground! He quickly turned and sprinted down the field, right past several Oregon defenders who thought the play was dead. "It hurts," said a dejected Pleasant. "It was just a crazy play."

Then, 37 yards later, Oregon defenders finally ran Dyer down and forced him out of bounds. But the damage was done. The play put Auburn in field goal range. They went on to kick a field goal on the final play of the game and win the national championship, 22 – 19.

PAYBACK

LSU vs. the University of Alabama

2012

When conference rivals LSU and Alabama met in the 2012 BCS National Championship Game, it marked the first rematch in BCS title game history. Earlier that season, the LSU Tigers had beaten the Crimson Tide in overtime, 9–6.

POWER CONFERENCES

Ten conferences make up the modern landscape of Division I football, along with a handful of independent schools such as Notre Dame. Leading the way are the Power Five conferences: the ACC, the Big Ten, the Big 12, the SEC, and the Pac-12.

Schools in these conferences generally field the best football teams in the country. But during the BCS era, one conference rose above all others. The SEC won nine of 16 titles during this time, including seven in a row from the 2006 to 2012 seasons.

Second-ranked Alabama was determined to exact revenge on first-ranked LSU in the title game, and that's exactly what they did. The Crimson Tide defense swarmed all over the field. LSU didn't even cross the 50-yard line in the first half, and they did so only once in the second half. In the entire game, they managed a mere five first downs! At the end, Alabama celebrated a dominating victory, 21–0, avenging their lone loss of the season and producing the only shutout in BCS National Championship Game history.

THIRD-STRING GOLD

Ohio State University vs. the University of Oregon

2015

The 2014 season was the first of the College Football Playoff era, and it proved a huge success with fans. In the semifinals, Oregon handed Florida State its first loss of the year, while Ohio State delivered a stunning defeat of Alabama. On January 12, 2015, the Buckeyes faced the Oregon Ducks for the first College Football Playoff National Championship.

Ohio State, the No. 4 seed entering the playoff, had seemed the longest of long shots to win it all. The Buckeyes had lost star quarterback Braxton Miller to injury before the season. Then, just before the team's conference championship game, second-string quarterback J. T. Barrett went down for the season. That left the Buckeyes with third-string passer Cardale Jones.

Jones didn't play like a third-stringer, though. First, he helped the Buckeyes to a dominating 59 – 0 win over Wisconsin in the conference championship to punch Ohio State's ticket into the playoff. Then he led the Buckeyes to an upset over the heavily favored Alabama Crimson Tide in the Sugar Bowl, which served as a playoff semifinal game.

Finally, Jones took the field against the Oregon Ducks in the first College Football Playoff National Championship. Jones's big arm, combined with the strong legs of running back Ezekiel Elliott, powered Ohio State to a convincing 42 – 20 victory and an unlikely national title.

5 CHALLENGES AND OPPORTUNITIES
THE FUTURE OF COLLEGE FOOTBALL

Modern college football would be all but unrecognizable to fans who witnessed the first game between Rutgers and Princeton in 1869. The sport has been transformed both on the field and off. Yet for all the advancements and changes, the game's future remains uncertain.

One of the biggest challenges college football will face in the years to come is the health and safety of its players. This is an issue for all levels of the sport, from peewee leagues to the NFL. Serious injuries have become a growing concern in football, especially head injuries. In 2013 the NFL and former players settled a lawsuit regarding the medical care provided to players who suffered concussions and other brain injuries during their professional careers. The NFL agreed to pay $765 million for medical care for former players. And yet many experts said that the money would not be enough to match the medical needs of injured players in the future.

Concussions and brain injuries are also common in the amateur ranks. According to statistics reported by the NCAA, from 2004 to 2009, more than 29,000 athletes were diagnosed with concussions received while playing major college athletics in the United States. More than half of those athletes were reported to be football players. Medical research has shown that concussions—especially multiple concussions—can have devastating long-term effects on mental health. The NCAA has little choice but to respond to this health issue. How can they keep players safe while maintaining the hard-hitting action that fans love?

Another major issue that college football will have to tackle in the years to come is player compensation. Unlike the NFL, where players are paid well for the risks they take, current rules state that college players can receive no money for their play. Athletes may receive scholarships, but the NCAA strictly monitors and enforces rules that prevent colleges and their supporters from compensating athletes in any other way.

These rules have recently come under fire. Major college football programs earn millions of dollars each year for their schools. Money flows in from ticket and merchandise sales, TV deals, and other avenues. Coaches take home multimillion-dollar salaries. Yet the athletes get no part of this massive windfall. Is it fair? Many athletes and others say no.

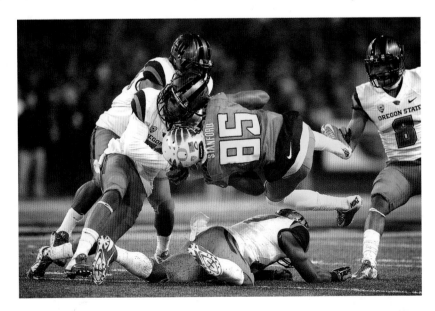

Despite modern safety gear, big hits like this can still cause serious injuries.

In 2014 members of Northwestern University's football team brought this issue to the forefront by voting to form a labor union—a move many believe could be the first step in seeing major college athletes treated more like employees and less like students. As an organized union, the Northwestern players will have more power to negotiate with the university on issues such as compensation and the way injured players are treated. "We're one step closer to a world where college athletes are not stuck with sports-related medical bills, do not lose their scholarships when they are injured, are not subject to unnecessary brain trauma, and are given better opportunities to complete their degree," said former Northwestern quarterback Kain Colter after the vote to form a union.

Other people disagree with Colter. They claim that these changes would harm smaller schools, which don't earn as much money from football as the major college

Fans loved the first College Football Playoff National Championship game in 2015.

The Ohio State Buckeyes surprised many people by winning the national championship in 2015.

programs do. Small schools could not pay athletes, resulting in the best football players going elsewhere. That could make for a handful of ultrapowerful teams and far less competitive balance than currently exists.

Despite these and other obstacles, fans are optimistic about the future. The 2014 season introduced the long-anticipated playoff system to largely positive reviews and a massive following—more than 33 million people watched the title game on ESPN, a record for a cable TV program. Most fans agreed that the College Football Playoff should put an end to split or controversial championships once and for all. For more than a century, college football's championship had been shrouded in controversy and uncertainty. Players, coaches, and fans alike look forward to a new era of college football, where the question "Who's No. 1?" is answered on the field each and every year.

SOURCE NOTES

22 Earl Gustkey, "The Most Memorable Rose Bowl—History: In the 1963 Game, Wisconsin, Led by Quarterback Ron Vander Kelen, Scored 23 Points in the Fourth Quarter in 42 – 37 Loss to USC," *Los Angeles Times*, January 1, 1992, http://articles.latimes.com/1992-01-01/sports/sp-1114_1_rose-bowl-game.

49 Izzy Gould, "Alabama News and Notes: Crimson Tide Returns to Practice Wednesday," *AL.com*, December 27, 2011, http://www.al.com/sports/index.ssf/2011/12/alabama_news_and_notes_crimson.html.

51 Jeff Merron, "The List: Gutsiest Calls in Sports," *ESPN.com*, accessed March 24, 2015, http://espn.go.com/page2/s/list/gutsiestcalls.html.

55 "Auburn Claims SEC's Fifth Straight National Title by Dropping Oregon on Late Field Goal," *ESPN.com*, January 10, 2011, http://scores.espn.go.com/ncf/recap?gameId=310102483.

60 "NU Players Cast Secret Ballots," *ESPN.com*, April 26, 2014, http://espn.go.com/chicago/college-football/story/_/id/10837584/northwestern-wildcats-players-vote-whether-form-first-union-college-athletes.

GLOSSARY

concussion: an injury to the brain

Heisman Trophy: an award given each season to the most outstanding college football player

integrate: to include people of all races

rugby: a team sport similar to football in which players score points by carrying the ball over the opposing team's goal line or by kicking it through goalposts

underdog: a team expected to lose a game

upset: a game in which an underdog wins

FURTHER READING

Books

Bowker, Paul. *Playing Pro Football*. Minneapolis: Lerner Publications, 2015.

Braun, Eric. *Super Football Infographics*. Minneapolis: Lerner Publications, 2015.

Diemer, Lauren. *Rose Bowl*. New York: AV2 by Weigl, 2014.

Gutman, Dan. *The Day Roy Riegels Ran the Wrong Way*. New York: Bloomsbury, 2011.

Van Pelt, Don, and Brian Wingate. *An Insider's Guide to Football*. New York: Rosen Central, 2015.

Weinreb, Michael. *Season of Saturdays: A History of College Football in 14 Games*. New York: Scribner, 2014.

Websites

College Football Playoff http://www.collegefootballplayoff.com
Learn more about the national championship at the official website of the College Football Playoff.

ESPN—College Football http://espn.go.com/college-football
Visit ESPN's college football page for scores, schedules, and much more.

NCAA Championship History http://www.ncaa.com/history/football/fbs
This NCAA website is the place to go for a complete list of college football's champions.

INDEX

ABOUT THE AUTHOR

Matt Doeden began his career as a sportswriter, covering everything from high school sports to the NFL. Since then he has written hundreds of children's and young adult books on topics ranging from history to sports to current events. His titles *Sandy Koufax, Tom Brady: Unlikely Champion,* and *The World Series: Baseball's Biggest Stage* were Junior Library Guild selections. His title *Darkness Everywhere: The Assassination of Mohandas Gandhi* was among the Best Children's Books of the Year by the Children's Book Committee at Bank Street College. Doeden, an avid football fan, lives in Minnesota with his wife and two children.

PHOTO ACKNOWLEDGMENTS

The images in this book are used with the permission of: © iStockphoto.com/ftwitty, (football texture); AP Photo/Cal Sport Media, pp. 4, 30; © Look and Learn/Illustrated Papers/Bridgeman Images, p. 6; © Saint Louis University, p. 9; © Stanford University Athletics, p. 11; AP Photo/Bettmann/Corbis, p. 12; AP Photo/Dave Martin, p. 16; AP Photo/Eric Draper, p. 17; AP Photo/Scott A. Miller, p. 18; © University Libraries Division of Special Collections, The University of Alabama, p. 21; AP Photo, pp. 23, 33, 38, 46; AP Photo/Mark J. Terrill, pp. 25, 53; AP Photo/Paul Sakuma, pp. 27, 28; AP Photo/Bettmann/Corbis, p. 34; © Collegiate Images/Getty Images, p. 35; © A.Y. Owen/The LIFE Images Collection/Getty Images, p. 37; AP Photo/Athlon Sports, p. 41; AP Photo/Tom Hauck, p. 43; AP Photo/Cal Sport Media, p. 44; AP Photo/John Raoux, p. 50; AP Photo/Doug Mills, p. 51; AP Photo/Paul Spinelli, p. 55; AP Photo/Troy Wayrynen, p. 59; AP Photo/Kevin Reece, p. 60; AP Photo/Ric Tapia, p. 61.

Front cover: © Kevin C. Cox/Getty Images (National Championship Game), © iStockphoto.com/ftwitty (football texture).

Flap: Manny Flores/Cal Sport Media/Newscom.